CW01024361

OVERCOMING THE SPIRIT OF FEAR AND WORRY

Oteng Montshiti

1

OVERCOMING THE SPIRIT OF FEAR AND WORRY

COPYRIGHT ©2020

CONTACT ADDRESS: OTENG MONTSHITI

P O BOX M1139

KANYE

BOTSWANA

E-MAIL ADDRESS: otengmontshiti@gmail.com

Contact number: (+267) 74 644 954

Table of contents

Acknowledgments

Writing a book is not an easy task. Therefore I would like to thank our Lord Jesus Christ, my family especially my lovely wife who supported me.

OVERCOMING FEAR

WHAT IS THE SPIRIT OF FEAR?

One day, on a dark night I was pacing along the dusty gravel road heading home from a place of entertainment. I felt as if somebody was following me, I ignored that. Then, I heard footsteps behind me. I halted on my tracks. Heart racing, flushed with fear and spun around and yelled,

"Who is there?" but it was so silent like the realm of the dead.

I continued walking throwing short glances around but the sound started again. My hair shot up on my head, my heart leaped to my throat and broke into a run. The sound of the footstep intensified. I shattered the stillness of the night with my voice. Suddenly, a dark figure appeared ahead of me, as it approaches me I released it was somebody I knew. I released a sigh of relief as I came to a skidding halt beside him. He asked me, "What is going on?" Then, I told him that somebody was following me. He glanced around investigating the surroundings but there was nothing. Suddenly, he laughed uncontrollably and stopped. He instructed me to walk around and the sound started.

"You see, it was the sound of your footsteps," I was face was flushed with shame.

"But..."

"No but, it is well with you," he said as he patted my back,

Do you see how dangerous the spirit of fear is?

Fear makes you see, hear, and feel things that are not there. While in actual fact, it is just your mind or imagination playing monkey tricks on you.

WHAT IS THE SPIRIT OF FEAR

Fear simply means to believe a lie. A lie opposes the truth.

It is the absence of faith because faith and fear can't dwell in the same heart or spirit. When faith comes into your heart fear fades away. If somebody says, "I believe in God but I am afraid of demons or evil spirits, he or she isn't telling the truth because you can't have faith and fear at the same time. When you have faith in God you become bold like a lion.

Fear is a spiritual force that the Devil uses to gain access to the lives of people. There is a simple rule in this world, whatever you fear is going to manifests in your life. For example, if you fear sickness it is going to manifest in your life, and so on.

Origin of the spirit of fear

2Timothy 1:7 For God hath not given us the spirit of fear; but of power, and of love, and of a sound mind.

Everything that happens under heaven or the sun originates somewhere in the unseen realm. There are two main sources namely; God and the devil. Fear is a spiritual tool that the devil uses to gain access to your life. But be of good cheer, God has given you the power to reject whatever comes or knocks at the door of your mind. Your mind has doors. When you embrace the spirit of fear it enters your spirit or mind and, torment you day and night. Any thought that you permit to dwell in your heart will rule over your life. For example, if fear rules you, you are going to live under constant pressure and serve pain.

However, at the opposite end lies the spirit of faith. It destroys fear. It believes in the impossible becoming possible. It originates from God. It is a spiritual tool that you use as a child of God to offer spiritual sacrifices like praise and worship unto the Lord.

Types of fear

They are two types of fear namely;

The fear of man

One day, a friend of mine told me that somebody wanted to partner with him in the business of cooking and selling food. He told me that he rolled that idea over and over in his mind and he concluded that he couldn't do business with that particular brother. I asked him, why he is throwing that opportunity away when it was hard to secure a sustainable job at that time. He told me that he is a degree holder and said;

"What do you think people are going to think about me," he asked.

I tried to give some sound advice but he turned me down. Today, the business is winning lucrative tenders and my friend regrets the decisions he took.

10

The above scenario is what is called the fear of man, when you have the fear of man you will always think about what other people might say or think about you. In life one thing is certain, you can't please everybody. There will always be people who bury their heads between their hands and laugh at you behind your back. In this world, you must learn to please yourself. Do you know why? It is because you are the only person who knows what you want out of life.

God can use small things that are despised by people around you to prepare you for the greater life ahead. For example, before I become a writer, I worked as a security guard and a laborer in the construction industry. I would supply bricklayers with mortar and bricks under the boiling sun of Africa. It was not easy because I am the product of college. I learned to put my qualification aside and lean on God for guidance. Today, have built a nice house for me without hiring people because of the knowledge and experience I acquired in the construction industry. If I could have allowed the fear of man to stand between me and God's preparation stage, I wouldn't have learned anything in life.

The fear of God

Proverbs 9:10 The fear of the LORD *is* the beginning of wisdom: and the knowledge of the holy *is* understanding.

The fear of God simply means to honor God in everything you do in life. It is to love Him with all your heart, soul, and spirit. If you have the fear of God you will not do anything that might hurt his feelings. Many people don't know that He has feelings like us, for example, He can be very happy or very sad depending on the kind of life you're living.

When you have the fear of God, you will do everything in truth and spirit. The word of God is the truth. Therefore, it simply

12

means to do things that are aligned with the word of God and under the influence of the Holy Spirit. Anything that is not in accordance with the word of God, please don't do it because it will hurt God's feelings.

The fear of God is to do things after consulting Him. That's to say, you must pray over every decision you make in life and get His approval. To learn more about the ways God uses to speak with us, you must read my book entitled: **Heavenly Whispers: How God speaks with us.** For example, during the election, you must ask Him to guide you to vote for a man or woman after His heart. You can get into fasting and prayer for his opinion. He is faithful he will reveal to you the person you should vote for. If His guidance is not being followed you can go and vote for people who are not after his heart. Somebody who is after His heart is a person who has the interest of his kingdom at heart. That's to say, somebody who wants the kingdom of God to expand on earth not somebody who wants to be voted into political office to fill up his or her belly.

What invites the spirit of fear into your life?

There are many things or activities that can invite the spirit of fear to attack you. It can attack you knowingly and unknowingly. As a child of God, you must be very vigilante or sensitive spiritually when the spirit of fear knocks at the door of your heart.

Watching and reading ungodly materials

One day, I watched a horror movie and I went to bed. Guess what happened, that night I had a streak of a nightmare. Do you know the reason behind that? It was because I fed my spirit with demonic contents. In this world there is a simple rule, whatever you watch is deposited into your spirit and it is going to tint your inner man or spirit with demonic stains that will manifest especially in your dreams. That's why you must watch and read Godly materials.

If you watch and read ungodly materials like pornographic videos and magazines you open the spiritual door for spiritual spouses to attack you. If you are spiritually sensitive or your consciousness is alive when you start to watch demonic things, sometimes you will be filled with the fear of God and you will hear a still small voice on the inside speaking to you to stop what you are doing.

Ungodly conversation

One day, I was in one of my neighbor's yard in the evening having discussions about things of darkness. We talked about the snakes of the caves which can change into various forms. For example, we said they could change into a beautiful white woman, a colorful flower, cows, and money, and so on. The topic changed to the issue of witchcraft. That's to say, how they operate in the demonic realm. Suddenly the spirit of fear struck my heart and I could hear a small voice telling me that I should start praying in my heart because I have I open the door for the demonic spirit in the unseen realm through our conversation and I covered myself with the blood of Jesus Christ. Then, I changed the topic to godly things and confidence and boldness sat in.

When I got home that night something started to walk on the roof of my house. I grabbed my Bible and prayed using Psalm 91 and the movement diminished. Ungodly conversations can open the door for the spirit of fear to attack you. Please, from today as a covenant child of God avoid them because they open the door for the spirit of fear to attack you in the unseen realm.

Idle mind

Proverbs 16:27 An ungodly man diggeth up evil: and in his lips *there is* as a burning fire.

The most dangerous person is somebody who has an idle mind. That's to say, somebody whose mind isn't too engaged on anything. An idle mind is like a car that is just idling. It's not moving. In life, you must discover something you are good at and do it. For example, if you are a good singer don't stay home and do nothing, find a singing group in the community, and engage your mind. You can join the local church and start singing for the glory of God.

If your mind isn't engaged Satan is going to target you. And the first thing he is going to do is to give you demonic or ungodly suggestions. The more you embrace them, is the more he fills your mind with fear. When fear has overtaken you he is going to torment your mind and spirit day and night.

Past experience

What has happened to you in the past can come back into the present and haunt you, especially if you are not a child of God. Satan can use your past experience to instill and inject the spirit of fear into your heart. Remember, where there is a spirit of fear there is no progress. People who live in that realm are always stagnated. In life, I have never seen anybody who is ruled by the spirit of fear progressing or overcoming situations.

Satan always brings your past mistakes into the present to condemns and use the tool of fear to torment you. If you don't rebuke or reject it he is going to cripple your creativity. For example, we were eight in my family. Two ladies and six men, five men have passed away and I am the only guy left in the family. One day, I became very sick guess what happened Satan started ministering to me.

"Yes, what killed your brothers is going to kill you"

The more I listened to his voice was the more fear entered my heart. I started imagining myself in the coffin being transported to the graveyard and lowered down into the grave. The spirit of fear struck through my imagination. My face was flushed with fear. Do you see now how your past experience can open the door for the spirit of fear to enter into your spirit or heart?

Background

The way you were brought up by elderly people can have a great influence on your life. Your background includes your culture, educational level, and social status. In my culture so many people believe in the power of witchcraft and such information has been handed from one generation to another. So many people in my community don't trust or love one another because they believe they will bewitch them. They don't know that there is a spiritual being in the unseen realm that is using such kind of information to fill them with fear and terror.

The level of your education can hinder or fill you with fearful thoughts when it comes to decision making. Today, people can't say, "I am sorry" because they are afraid that people are going to laugh at them because they are well learned. However, when you are with God put your educational level or qualifications aside and solely depend upon the Lord for guidance and wisdom. Your background doesn't matter before Him, If your father died because of a heart attack, fear not you will not die from that. The Lord is with you. If your mother is a poor person when you are with Him, He is going to rewrite your story for your family. *SO FEAR NOT!!!*

Deuteronomy 31:8 And the LORD, he *it is* that doth go before thee; he will be with thee, he will not fail thee, neither forsake thee: fear not, neither be dismayed.

What causes the spirit of worry?

Worrying about tomorrow

Matthew 6:25 Therefore I say unto you, Take no thought for your life, what ye shall eat, or what ye shall drink; nor yet for your body, what ye shall put on. Is not the life more than meat, and the body than raiment?

Matthew 6:26 Behold the fowls of the air: for they sow not, neither do they reap, nor gather into barns; yet your heavenly Father feedeth them. Are ye not much better than they?

Matthew 6:34 Take therefore no thought for the morrow: for the morrow shall take thought for the things of itself.

In life, you must learn to be content with God's provision for today. The moment you start to think about what you are going to eat, wear, and where you are going to sleep tomorrow you are opening the door for the Devil to inject your spirit with worry and fear. Just relax and take out a step of faith today God will provide for you or take care of the rest.

Remember, tomorrow supply doesn't come from you but from the throne of

God. The bible says God is the provider, not you. Provision comes from God and your role is to walk in obedience with Him. Obedience is the master in your spiritual walk with Him. If you walk in obedience you shouldn't worry about anything because he is in control of everything concerning your life.

If you read the word of God from Genesis to Revelation you will learn about great men and women of God who walked in accordance with the instructions of God, putting worries aside knowing that the creator of heaven and earth is in control. Remember God cloth flowers with colorful garments and provide for the birds daily but they don't plant anything. What about you his greatest product created in His image?

Don't worry about anything in life no matter what life throws at you. Challenges are not there to inject you with worry but with strength. Everything that comes across your path is for your good. In the word of God, everything works for good for those who love the Lord and are called according to his purpose. You see, there is nothing to worry about.

Whether it is a satanic storm or not just you should slide back in the passenger's seat and watch God taking care of that situation. He is going to use that storm to strengthen you. Worry not the creator of heaven and earth is on the throne and he has your future in his hands. Remember God said He will be with you even unto the end of the earth so focus on Him and put worries aside. The more you focus on him is the more worry fades away and his peace sets in.

Your tomorrow is a mystery only known by God. To be in good health tomorrow it is because of his goodness. Trust God because he has taken care of you in the past and will do it again tomorrow. The flowers fall but his goodness lasts forever.

How to overcome the spirit of fear and worry

Declare the scriptures

Before I become born again I was very shy and afraid of speaking in front of people. During my schooling days, I would be chosen by teachers as a class leader and I would turn them down. I was even afraid to speak in front of a group of people. Guess what happened! I met a certain brethren in the Lord who told me that I must personalize the scriptures and declare them.

I went ahead in obedience and started to declare the word of God whenever fear struck my heart. My favorite verse was 2 Timothy 1: 7 and I would declare;

"God you haven't given me the spirit of fear but you have given me the spirit of a sound mind and boldness. Today, by your

25

special grace I am going to lead people in prayer."

As I continue to declare the scriptures like that, the spirit of fear started to diminish in my life, and boldness set in. Today, I am free from the spirit of fear and what God has done for me he can do it for you.

Be bold

Declaring the scriptures without corresponding action is waste of time. The next step is to take a bold step and face your fear. In life, unless you come out of the comfort zone and confront your fear you will never enjoy the fruits of freedom. If you are afraid of speaking in front of a huge crowd you must declare the relevant scriptures and start to attend social gatherings like weddings and funerals. As you do that the spirit of fear is being broken in your heart. If you persist boldness will set in.

26

2Timothy 1:7 For God hath not given us the spirit of fear; but of power, and of love, and of a sound mind.

If you want somebody to marry but you are afraid of approaching sisters start to approach them and speak your mind or propose to them. If they mock you it is fine, because in life practice makes perfect. I am not saying go around and sleep with them, I am saying propose them, and as you do that the spirit of fear will be broken down. Remember, breaking from the spirit of fear is a process and personal responsibility. It isn't all up to God you have a role to play.

Maintain your ground on the word of God

In this world, everybody wants to be happy and to have inner peace. In the search for freedom and peace of mind, there are things that can happen to you that can provoke the spirit of worry, fear, and steal your peace. As I have said earlier, whatever happens to your mind doesn't matter what matters is how you react to situations and challenges that life throws at you. Your thinking ability can be crippled or impaired by the spirit of worry and fear.

One day, my mother decided to give me one of her plots, when we approached the land board authority we ran from pillar to post for over eight years. During that time frame, worry started to creep into my heart. I started to wonder whether they were going to give me the plot or not. Because their statements were not consistent and suspected that an act of fraud had taken place. Worry ate up every piece of my heart. During the night I would stare blankly at the roofing sheets, twist and turn on my bed. My peace was stolen.

As time progressed, I became short-tempered. I would snap at everybody over small matters. One day, something flashed through my mind and told me that

28

I should hand my problems to the Lord otherwise I would run mad or went the graveyards too early. God was busy working out the answers in the unseen realm.

From that time onwards, I learned to put my strength, wisdom aside, and lean on God. That's to say, I handed my predicament unto to God. Oh my God, my inner peace was restored, and started to sleep like a baby at night. I focused on other areas of my life and only phoned them or went there to make follow-ups. That's what is called handing your problems to the Lord.

Prayer item

God, I thank you. You are the King of glory. Thank you, Lord, for taking care of tomorrow. God, you are on the throne. God, you are the provider, and give me the grace to depend on your provision for today and let tomorrow be.

I stand against the spirit of fear and worry in the spirit even in the physical. Lord whatever the spirit of fear and worry has destroyed in my life be restored, in Jesus Christ might name, Amen.

Prophetic declaration

God I am free from the spirit of fear and worry

Father all the areas are restored

God, I will not borrow garments because worry and fear I shall be a lender

I am blessed forever, Amen.

Celebrate your victory over the spirit of fear and worry

You are free from the spirit of fear and worry in Jesus Christ's mighty name.

Shalom!!!

THE END

Books by the same author

Provoking the supernatural through faith

Provoking the supernatural through prayer

Provoking the supernatural through prayers and spiritual battles

Heavenly whispers: How God speaks with us

Meditations made simple: how to meditate upon the word of God or his promises

Overcoming challenges

God according to Psalm 23

The dimension of miracles and blessings

Beyond the sinking sun

Financial freedom

Heaven is your limit

The power of the spoken words

If you can see it the power is available to achieve it

Principles of an eagle

Lightning Source UK Ltd.
Milton Keynes UK
UKRC021233141220
375018UK00011B/202